Book 4

MY FUN-TO-READ BOOKS

Stories for enjoyment and enrichment

Text adapted by James Ertel

THE SOUTHWESTERN COMPANY • Nashville

LIFE
IN THE
FOREST

Illustrations by Edwin Huff

THE SOUTHWESTERN COMPANY • Nashville

The *True-to-Life* photographs in this book are based on the educational motion picture, "Life in the Forest," produced by Encyclopaedia Britannica Films, Inc., and photographed by William A. Anderson. Scenes for this film were taken over a period of many months and in many different parts of the United States. The forest depicted in this film is actually a composite forest, one made up of features of many different kinds of forests.

The design of this book is by Ruth Rooney.

This is the Forest. Many kinds of
plants and animals live here.
    Each of these things depends in
some way on each of the others.

A forest changes.

A young forest has mostly aspens and poplars and shrubs. These trees and shrubs change the soil and help it hold more water.

In time, pines take over. The pine trees change the soil still more. Finally beech, oak, and maple trees can grow there.

Trees give food and shelter to many birds and animals.

The plants of the forest help make the forest beautiful. Wild daisies grow in forest clearings. The bright jack-in-the-pulpits grow in shady places. Light-green ferns grow in the damp places.

Forest animals that eat plants look for new plants in the spring. Many of these forest animals are not only hungry, but also skinny after the long winter.

When the skunk cabbage comes up in early spring, bears dig it up and eat it.

The early plants are hungrily eaten by deer. They are tired of having to eat twigs and bark all winter.

Rabbits live in or near forests. They depend on speed to escape from the animals which like to eat them.

Cottontail rabbits live at the edges of forests. On moonlight nights, many of them gather in a clearing. There they eat and play together.

The enemies of rabbits are foxes,
bobcats, snakes, and large birds. Rabbits
are always in danger.

A chipmunk spends most of his life gathering food.

He starts to store grain, nuts and seeds in early summer. By winter he has gathered so much that his store rooms are filled with it.

The frisky chipmunk digs underground tunnels and rooms. Usually, each chipmunk has his own home. However, in a bad winter, one chipmunk may let friends move in with him.

The main entrance to a chipmunk home is often at the base of a tree. Off the main tunnel are store rooms, bedrooms, and emergency exits.

Gray squirrels are around all year in the forest. They are always out looking for a meal.

Instead of filling store rooms with nuts, the gray squirrel buries each nut separately in a shallow hole. In winter, the squirrel looks for his buried nuts. He never finds many of them. They later grow up to be trees.

Most forest animals are quiet. The red squirrel is not.

If any strange animal is in a red squirrel's territory, it makes a terrible racket. It chatters and squawks and fills the forest with noise.

A muskrat house in a pond usually
looks like a sloppy beaver house.
    If it seems like a good idea at the
time, a muskrat may decide to store a few
roots and bulbs. Usually, he doesn't
bother.

Muskrats do not get along well with each other. Each one fights hard for his own territory.

Sometimes, but not often, several muskrats will live together.

Whitetail deer do not have as many enemies as they used to have. Years ago wolves killed many deer. Today the wolves are gone.

Each mother deer has many babies during her life. She may have two or three each year.

In the morning, the mother hides her
babies before she goes off to feed. They lie
absolutely still all day.

Their coloring makes them hard to see.
In the evening, the mother comes back to her
babies and guards them through the night.

Caribou are members of the deer family.
They are also called reindeer.

The moose is the biggest member of the
deer family. Many people think he is also
the most ugly member of that family.

Elks are members of the deer family.
Male elks have big antlers and often fight
each other.

Weasels are small, fast, fierce animals. They are meat eaters, and are always looking for mice and small rabbits to eat.

A weasel is small enough to chase a mouse into its hole.

In places where it snows a lot, the weasel changes color. His brown summer fur turns to pure white fur.

Weasel life is not easy. Ten babies may be born at one time. It is a hard job for the parents to find food for that many.

A raccoon likes a home near water. He would like a hollow tree, but if he can't find one, he will live in a hole in the ground or in a small cave.

A raccoon eats vegetables and fruits, frogs, fish, and mice.

Raccoons like water not only because
they find food there, but also because
they like to wash their food before they
eat it.

A raccoon is not strong, and he is not
fast. But he is smart, and that helps him
escape his enemies.

The skunk is left alone by most forest animals. The skunk has a stinking spray.

This terrible smell seems to make the skunk feel safe. The skunk walks slowly through the forest. He could run if he wanted, but he is just not afraid.

Most skunks live along the forest
edge where there are plenty of mice and
insects. One of the favorite foods of a
skunk is turtle eggs.

Usually, four to six baby skunks are
born. The father brings food and leaves
it at the den entrance. He is not allowed
inside. He has to sleep outside.

A fox likes to live along the edge of a forest.

Foxes will eat almost anything. They eat fruits and vegetables, nuts, small animals, and even insects.

Foxes come in different colors. There are red ones, black ones, silver ones, and red ones with black stripes.

The tail of a fox is large
and beautiful. In the quick
turns of a chase, it helps him
keep his balance.

A bobcat eats mice, rabbits and birds.
If he is very hungry, he will eat a skunk.
A bobcat has a nasty temper.

   Once in a while a bobcat will climb a
tree. He can swim if he has to, but he
would rather not.

Bobcats usually live in a hollow log, or in a cave. Babies usually come three or four at a time.

Baby bobcats have spots. The spots go away when they get older.

Bears sleep through the coldest part of the winter. Mothers expecting babies find a good den and make a bed of leaves and grass.

Baby bears are born in winter.

The babies live on the fat their mother stored up in the summer. Her body turns this fat into milk.

If she ate roots, berries, fruit, mice and fish, her milk will be good. But if she ate candy bars, ice cream, and garbage, her milk will be poor.

The forest is a place where plants and animals depend on each other. Some forest plants cannot live anywhere else.

The forest is a place of battles. Smaller animals are eaten by bigger animals.

The forest is also a place of peace. There is quiet and beauty. When a person goes into a forest, he should respect all the things that live there.

LIFE
ALONG THE
SEASHORE

Illustrations by Ruth Rooney

THE SOUTHWESTERN COMPANY • Nashville

Many of the true-to-life photographs in this book are taken from the educational filmstrip series "Classification of Invertebrate Animals," produced by Encyclopaedia Britannica Films, Inc. They are the work of the following photographers: Ron Church, Charles Huntington, Weldon Johnson, David C. Nicholson, Edward E. Palinscar, Rupert J. M. Riedl and Michael Wotton. Other photographs in the book were taken by Alan Solem, Jean Thomson and Bill Anderson. Mr. Anderson's photographs are related to the educational motion picture "Beach and Sea Animals," which he produced for Encyclopaedia Britannica Films, Inc. We wish to thank Marine Studios, Marineland, Florida, for their co-operation.

The design of this book is by Ruth Rooney. Supervision of color reproduction is by James Lockhart.

The seashore is a place where the ocean meets the land. It is a place where many unusual plants and animals live. Twice each day water covers, then uncovers the shore edges as the tide rises and falls.

On rocky shores there are hollow
places. When the tide goes out,
these hollows become still pools.
　　Many plants and animals live in
the rock pools. There are crabs,
fish, seaweeds, and other things.

Sea gulls walk from one rock pool to another at low tide.

Even hard-shelled crabs and clams are not safe from a gull. The gull will carry a crab or clam high into the air and drop it on a rock.

The shell of the crab or clam breaks. The gull flies down and eats the soft meat.

Small snails are also busy hunters in the rock pools. They crawl around on the rocks eating small barnacles.

Each snail has a long tongue covered with tiny teeth. The snail can push its tongue into the opening of a barnacle to eat it.

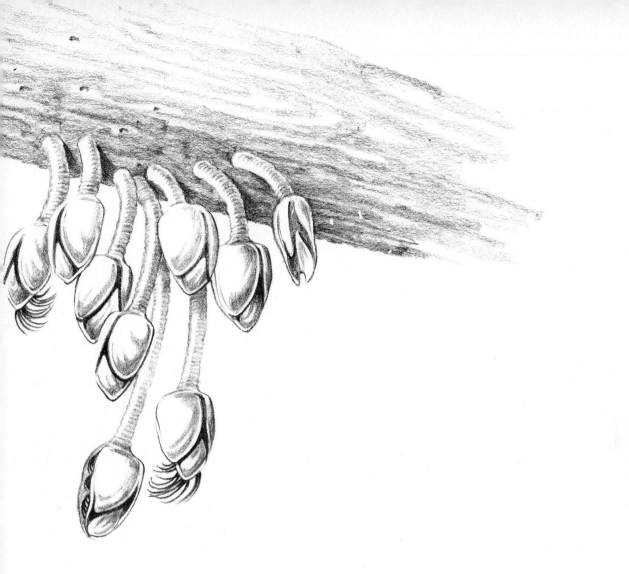

Barnacles spend their lives
fastened to one spot. They eat
very tiny plants and animals
that are in the water.

A barnacle has feathery arms
which jerk in and out, bringing
food to the barnacle's mouth.

Sea anemones look like flowers
in a rock pool. They are really fish-
eating animals.

The pretty petals of an anemone
are loaded with a poison. This poison
can kill a fish.

When an anemone kills a fish, the petals—
called tentacles—grab it.
The tentacles pull the fish into the
anemone's mouth.

Anemones can move, but not very fast.
A speed of three inches an hour is fast
for an anemone!

Starfish move through rock pools
on their five "arms."
A starfish can pull open a clam
shell with its arms. When the shell
is open, the starfish eats the clam.

Blue crabs scoot through the
rock pools looking for food. A blue
crab usually eats leftovers from
the meals of other animals.

All crabs have a hard shell. As
a crab grows, it changes its shell.
A new shell grows under the old
one. The old one splits open and
the crab wiggles out.

Clams live in rock pools, and in shallow parts of the sea. They spend their lives fastened to a rock. Only the heaviest waves can tear them loose.

Clams die if they are torn loose and cast up on the shore.

Shearwaters are sea birds. They can swim under water to catch fish.

Shearwaters eat small fish. These small fish eat much smaller sea animals.

The smallest animals eat the tiny plants of the sea. Sea plants are the basic food which all animal life in the sea depends on.

Mangrove swamps are in warm seas. The long roots of mangrove trees go into the water.

Small sea animals like to hide in mangrove swamps. Bigger animals cannot get at them there.

Sea birds like to nest in mangrove trees.

Horseshoe crabs live in mangrove
swamps. These animals were on
earth before the dinosaurs were.
    The shell of this crab looks like
a horseshoe. That is how he got
his name.

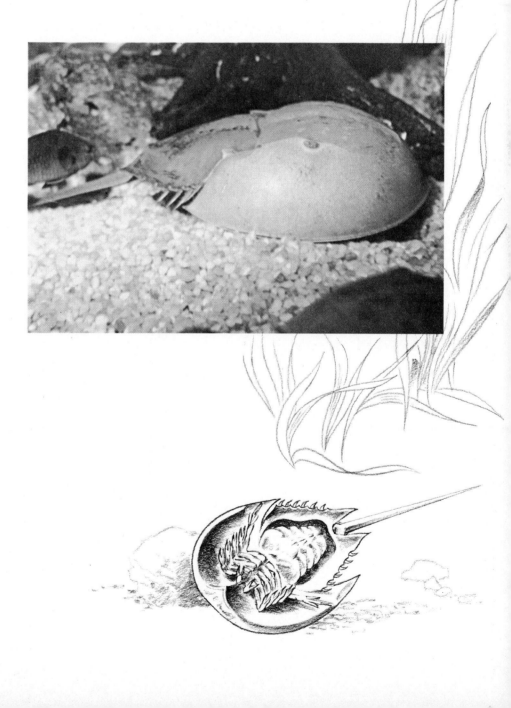

Hermit crabs like to live in mangrove swamps. To protect itself, a hermit crab looks for an empty snail shell, and backs into it.

Baby hermit crabs use very small snail shells. As they grow, they move into larger snail shells.

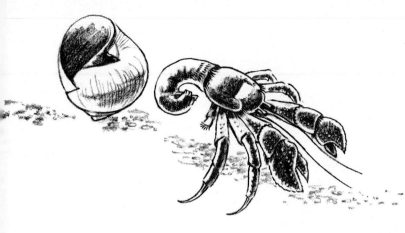

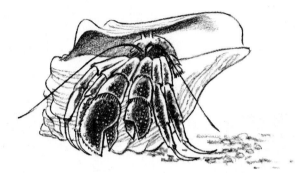

Beautiful avocets visit the mangrove swamps in the spring and
fall. They wade in the shallow
water and grab shrimps and worms
for food.

Tropical seas have palm trees growing along their shores. In the water are the strangest and most colorful sea animals in the world.

The beaches of tropical seas have many beautiful shells brought in by the waves.

Animals called sea urchins
live in tropical seas. They
crawl along the bottom of the
sea, looking for food.

Most sea urchins are round
and have sharp spikes. These
spikes are a safe place for
small fish to hide. Bigger
fish cannot catch them there.

The most beautiful clams
and snails live in tropical seas.
    Only a few kinds of clams can
swim. The file shell is one.
It swims by quickly opening
and closing the two parts of its
shell. It looks weird when it swims.

A snail shell is all one piece.
A snail can go inside it and close
the door.

　　This door is the hard bottom
of its one foot.

Land worms are not very pretty,
but some sea worms are. Some have
bright red arms that they use to
bring food to their mouths.

There are thousands of kinds of
worms in the sea. Some always stay
in one place. Some crawl along the
bottom of the sea. Some dig into
the mud of the sea bottom.

There are thousands of kinds of snails
in the sea. One of the prettiest is called
a flamingo tongue.

There are so many animals on the
sea bottom, that in some places it looks
like a garden.

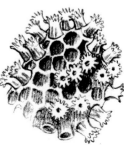

A sea horse is really a tiny fish.
Its head looks like a horse.

A sea horse can swim, but usually
it stays in one place. It holds onto a
plant stem with its tail.

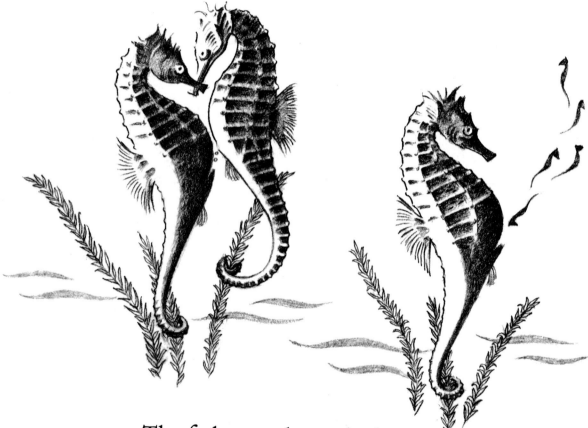

The father sea horse is the one
who takes care of the eggs. The
mother lays her eggs in a pouch in
the father's body.

After several weeks the eggs hatch
and the babies swim out. There may
be as many as 150 babies. They do
not all live.

The shallow sea has many bright colors and strange sights.

A bright red clam opens its shell, then swims away.

A giant snail crawls among bright orange sponges. On its back is an anemone almost as big as the snail.

Other animals, called oaten-pipes, put out tiny arms to catch food.

Sea turtles are some of the biggest
sea animals.

A female turtle lays her eggs on the beach.
She digs a shallow nest with her hind feet,
and buries her eggs in the sand.

In a few weeks, the tiny turtles are
born. They quickly run to the sea.

Jellyfish and Portuguese-men-of-war float on top of the sea.

Sometimes a strong wind will blow jellyfish onto a beach. They shrink up and die in the sun.

Hanging down from a jelly-fish are long threads. Some may be 100 feet long. These threads have a stinging poison, which can kill fish.

Corals live in warm tropical
seas. They are tiny animals who
build hard skeletons of lime
around themselves.

New corals build skeletons on
top of old corals who have died. Over
many hundreds of years, billions of

corals have built great reefs under
water. Some of these reefs are
hundreds of miles long.

Millions of small sea creatures
live among the corals. Larger
creatures cannot get at them there.

Some fish have strong teeth and
jaws. They can eat the hard corals.

Sergeant majors are bright colored
fish. They live near the corals
for protection.

The sea world is very different
from the land world. The sea world has
millions of kinds of creatures. Each creature
has its own way of living.

This wonderful sea world is little known
to man. There is much you can discover
by walking along a seashore or looking
into a rock pool.

Birds
in
summer

Drawings by EDWIN HUFF

THE SOUTHWESTERN COMPANY
Nashville

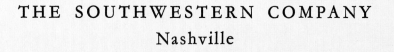

Many of the true-to-life photographs in this book are taken from the educational filmstrip series "Classification of Living Birds," produced by Encyclopaedia Britannica Films, Inc. These and others in the book are the work of the following photographers: Arthur A. Allen, Bill Anderson, James Beebe, Beecher Berry, Lynwood Chace, Norman Flitters, Kathleen Hodges, Weldon Johnson, David Lockhart, James Nessle and Michael Wotton. Encyclopaedia Britannica Press is indebted to Michigan Conservation Department for the photograph on this page.

The design of this book is by Alex D'Amato and Edwin Huff. Supervision of color reproduction is by James Lockhart.

Summer is coming when the winter ice
starts to melt. Grass turns green, and
new leaves grow on the trees.

Birds come back to the north. They
come from the warm south where they
lived during the winter.

Some birds travel in large flocks. Canada geese fly in large flocks across the sky spread out in a large V. They honk a lot when they fly.

They stop to rest and eat sometimes on a cold lake or pond. They are big birds, and can fill up a pond pretty fast.

Food is something birds are always looking for.

A woodpecker hunts in the trees for insects. Its strong beak can punch holes in a tree.

Robins hop in the fresh grass hunting worms. Later in the summer robins eat fruit. Fruit tastes better than worms.

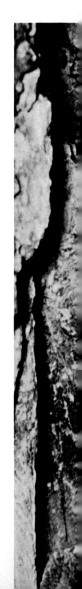

The nighthawk hunts for food in
the sky. It catches insects in the air.
It has a big mouth.

Nighthawks scream a lot as they fly.
Maybe you would scream a lot, too,
if you had to eat bugs.

A tufted titmouse has strong claws.
It can walk upside-down on twigs or up
and down the trunk of a tree.

In summer it eats caterpillars and
other insects. In winter it eats nuts.

Bird nests are of many different
sizes and shapes. Each kind of bird
builds its own kind of nest.

A robin nest is built of twigs, weed
stems, and even string, rags or paper.
These things are held together by mud.
The robin carries the mud to the nest
in its beak.

Robins like to build their nests in trees.

Barn swallows build their nests with mud and grass. They line them with very soft grass or feathers.

Sometimes sixty pairs of barn swallows may build nests in one barn.

A towhee builds its nest in bushes near the ground. The nest is made of stems, leaves and grass lined with soft grass and hair.

The killdeer lives in open fields. It often makes its nest right on the ground. It is usually made of pebbles or grass.

Gannets are sea birds. They build their nests on cliffs by the sea.

So many of them build their nests so close together that nobody knows how a gannet knows where its nest is. Gannets seem to know.

Canada geese build nests by a lake or pond. A father goose will fight hard to protect the eggs.

The screech owl's nest is hidden in a hollow tree.

During the day the mother sits on her white eggs. The father sits in a nearby tree.

Screech owls are night birds. At night, both parents hunt for mice, insects and small birds.

Eggs hatch after a few days.
Baby birds have a bump on their
beak. This bump is called an egg
tooth. They use this egg tooth to
break open their shell.

Most baby birds have no
feathers. Their eyes are closed and
they cannot see.

The mother and father
are very busy after the babies hatch.

The babies need food. They
need lots of it. The parents
have to find it and bring it to
the babies.

Brown thrasher babies like to eat insects. The parent thrashers eat fruit most of the time. But they hunt for insects for their babies.

Parent thrashers raise two families during a summer.

Parent thrashers must be very tired by the end of the summer.

The mother and father vireo
take turns sitting on the eggs.
When he sits on the nest, the father
sings all the time. Most birds do
not do that.

Vireos sing all day during the
summer. They are almost never quiet.

Mockingbirds raise two or three families in a summer. They are kept busy, but they still manage to sing a lot.

The mockingbird got its name because it likes to imitate the song of other birds. It is a very good singer.

Young terns are born in nests along
the seashore. They can hop after a day
or two. It takes many more weeks for
them to get strong enough to fly.

Baby terns stand at the edge of the
sea and watch their parents. The parents
fly out over the water looking for fish.

Baby mourning doves hatch in a nest in a tree. They stay in the nest until they are ready to fly.

Mourning doves are found all across the United States. They look a little like pigeons, but they are not pigeons.

Cedar waxwing babies are
fed insects for the first day or two
of their lives. After that they
eat berries.

With all those wide-open mouths
in front of her, it must be hard for
a mother waxwing to decide which
one to feed. Mother birds seem
to know, however.

Kingfisher babies are fed whole fish. Sometimes the fish is almost as long as the baby.

Kingfishers seem to like cold weather. In the winter they go just far enough south to find unfrozen water where they can fish. They fly back north in early spring.

Young ducks are able to walk and
swim on the same day they hatch.

Young wood ducks hatch in a nest
in a hole in a tree. They jump out and
float down to the ground.

The mother leads the ducklings to
the nearest water. The ducklings swim
at once. The mother teaches them
how to find food.

Young owls stay in their nest in a hole in a tree until they are ready to fly.

At first the parents feed the babies pieces of dead mice. Later the parents feed them whole animals.

Owls have big eyes.

Leaving the nest is a very
big change for young birds. Their
wing feathers are not fully grown.
They cannot fly very well.

During the last days in their
nest in a hole in a tree, young
crested flycatchers stand near the
entrance of the hole.

At last they come out and
perch in a row on a branch.

After a young bluejay leaves the nest, it perches in some bushes. It waits to be fed.

After a while, it begins to follow the parent. As it gets stronger, the young jay starts to find its own food.

Sometimes a young bird does not want to leave its nest.

Then the parents go to work. They may try to scare him out.

If that does not work, they coax him out. They bring food, then hop a little way off.

The young bird follows. The parents go a little farther, and the young one follows again.

The parents of young birds teach them how to keep out of danger. If a cat is near, the parents call the young to a safe place.

Parents also teach the young birds where they can be safe. Wild ducks or geese learn that they are safe from hunters on certain ponds and marshes.

When summer leaves start
to fall, most birds fly south.

It has been a busy summer.
They built nests, hatched eggs,
and raised children. They will
rest through the winter. Next
summer they will be back.